Sculpting Fire

A Poetic Journey
Into Blasphemy
at the
Turn of the
21st Century

Sculpting
Fire

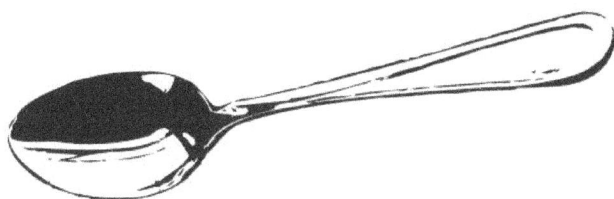

A Poetic Journey
Into Blasphemy
at the
Turn of the
21st Century

By
Keith Hell

Published by BMF.publishing, LLC

Edited by Qua and BMF.publishing, LLC

Cover Art by Qua

BMF. Publishing, LLC
P.O. Box 2248
Thomasville, NC 27361

304-553-5807

ISBN-13:978-0996032810 (BMF.publishing, LLC)
ISBN-10:0996032819

Table of Contents

Preface

Sculpting Fire: A Poetic Journey Into Blasphemy at the Turn of the 21st Century is a fragmented, sometimes chaotic look into a life that most people today have never experienced and few could ever fully understand.

Written during an isolated and harsh existence, this book is a hammer of reality that not only happened to Keith, but still happens to a surprising number of people in impoverished areas. It depicts a largely ignored demographic in America: the poor rural youths who never had a chance to dream of a quiet life, pension or a pile of grandbabies. Keith will be the first to admit that he never dreamed of living to see his thirtieth birthday. It is a glimpse at a world where you know, almost from birth, that the deck is stacked against you. It is about what happens when you make a few poor choices in a small, politically corrupt town. And perhaps most importantly, this book is an example of how words can become a conduit for escape in the midst of sheer madness.

Stylistic choices have been left mostly intact from the original journals. I encourage you to read closely, as each word and phrase was a very deliberate decision. It will reveal some scary truths and harsh realities about addiction, prison, and the path that leads an individual to these places. If you are a person who bets against the odds then please enjoy, because this is a book that never should have been completed.

Yet it was.

—*Qua*

Dedicated to Jackson

Untitled

How can the two coexist…the physical and the metaphysics
of the mind?
From hand to paper and the actions between become poetry
That internal shell of a man that stumbles in the spectrum of
images among images
Thousands of sweet little heartbreak burning fools of faith
In the stirrups and between the wings of a mass artistic
disaster
And you can unhinge those spinning gadgets of lust
The cells of my body and the sperm in which I lay naked
You can feast in the name of revolt
Tasting the nectars of war and what a god may bring you as
his host

I mewl to the politics of the Heiress, designer, mammoth
hunter
That certain one I loved long ago
Through a symbolic sexual encounter with a queen
succubus
I learned for the first time how to construct great music with
a symphony of beasts
And that became my first stand against such a great cunning
enemy of this world

With wails and shrieks of flaming heartache that pound in
low keys of loneliness
This is a world where I be the vampire phantom and my
entire universe be a violent Mecca of devastating poetry
It haunts with whispers from calamity's cold cobalt tomb

And in that place I became one with the very chemical drive
that shuttered my
brain
The one who kick-starts and confronts that pure white page
When the ink puddles and collects meaning and expression
at 3:30 in the morning
With sensitivities run rampant in red eyed slumber,
hypnotized by the word
Ash…embers…vapors to dew
The tongue hot and dry as the dust in Hell
Blissful and raging
Like dams of quivering orgasms
Flowing with pride and ego and suicides of ideas

Then enters those pin hole lights of dawn
That napalm the shadows slowly
You forget who your enemy has become
You question all great things and beings before you
You form opinions of life and love and death
And those there of that dream with you
The world becomes heavy with desire
And rest is a weary skeletal frame of pen.

Poetry Is

Poetry is endless
Poetry is nameless
Poetry is speechless
Poetry is unseen, untold, it is still not known
Poetry can drive you mad
Poetry carries her pulsating through my skull my vein my
tongue and eye
Poetry is me you all of the above, below, inside and out

Poetry is God's hand and the devil's foot
Poetry was born behind the brain
Before the first reflection of the sun
Before the glimpse of the first full moon

Poetry is sick
Poetry is fulfilling
Poetry is empty
Poetry is always yet never can be
Poetry is the spine of a million musicians
Poetry is straight
Poetry is gay
Poetry is bipolar

It is as cold as the winter's bones and as hot as the summers flesh
It is spiteful, deceitful, heroic yet shameful
It is the pupil of the soul
It is the ass of the lamb and grip of the wheel at a thousand miles an hour
Poetry is a good lick
It is the venom within the fang
Poetry is still sick
Poetry is the bastard hybrid of thought embodied by the mind
It is the skeletons dangling in the closet

Poetry is as bright as a one hundred watt bulb in a dark cement jail cell
Poetry is tired yet restless
Poetry is as comfortable as a daisy under a vulture's wing
It is fifty migs of morphine that pulsates a thousand times stronger
Poetry is coffee in the middle of the night
It is black, white, green, and blue
It is the octagon in the middle of a square
It is a bull without the horns

Poetry is the mother the father the semen and the corpse
Poetry is higher or lower depending on your calorie needs
It contains less than two percent of salt and only one gram of sugar daily
Poetry is the ringing of church bells on a Sunday morning
It is the dreaded last call on a Friday night
Poetry is a trapped prayer hovering in the stench of a bus station bathroom

It is the graffiti on the wall in an alley of murdered secrets
It is the dust on an antique
It is the smell of a whisper from a distant ghost
It is the ghost of the senses

It is the birth of the word beyond the letter
It is the asylum and the freedom
Poetry is as holy as Ginsberg and as unholy as De Sade
It is the pillow of the muscle ripening on the vine
It is time and space
Poetry is the heart crucified on the cross for all of our sins
and pleasures
Poetry is the problem that confides in the answer
It is the ancient Zen of a question you must not ask
Poetry is the death of the poet

Dedicated to Brian Johnson
SWR Jail, Fall 2005

Can You Find Me?

Can you find me?
In those Carolina nights
When I walked through the eyes of tornados
Only to come out unharmed on the other side
Standing face to face with a new companion
Who would take my hand and lead me straight to the smoky
distortions of Hell
Then abandoned me there, sky-walking naked

Can you find me?
Beneath the dark, oiled night sky
Where I thought I was touching the rim of the void
With my spider spinning speech you enjoyed and said you
understood

Can you find me?
Ankle high in the cold sad clay of a warm Jesus June
Before the death of me the first time
Before the baby screams
Before the upheaval of the slut brigade
Before they marched up the corduroy pant legs leaving jizm
in the lonesome cavity of the crotch

Can you find me?
On a Columbus Sunday in a telepathic car
Bathing in the crisp cool clouds of hysterical trips
Out in the woods
Walking backwards on tops of frozen streams
Reflecting a worn putrid face of downed redemptions

Can you find me?
Under panic drenched gurneys and hospital straps
Letting me shellac myself with human glycerin
While everyone became possessed by the devil
'til I reflected back home
Tail between legs
Begging for a reality beyond a writer

Can you find me?
Driving my punk blues all the way to emptiness
With a feline my only friend to trust
Living in grey wooden Pontiacs from summer to winter
A ricochet in the flux of pandemonium

Can you find me?
Developing habitual acts that would haunt me 'til this day
'Til I can revel in the flesh of my time
Blowing tar-stained trumpets
That announce I'm still alive
To ride the thunder of the new atom until tomorrow

Can you find me?
Before the giant monsters of emotion
Before the tides
Before the deranged astral solitudes of abandonment
Before the first violent sword was swung

Can you find me?
Before the great grin of officer swine
Who dined on my ass in a lucid courtroom
A buffet of exotic crimes under a dim ceiling of crooks

Can you find me?
When you searched below the floorboards of the earth
Crazed like Ugandan headhunters
With drooling erections in holsters
Thirsting for my throat
While my demise may grieve itself

Can you find me?
Hidden in the narrow chamber
Where that girl stood poised by the rush of morphine
And she helped you pull the trigger
Leaving me a million miles an hour
Glancing through the delicate china shop of loves boutique

Can you find me?
Scoring a fix off the highest hit-and-miss on dregs street
Back and forth
Off the shimmering lightning flash of my own nucleus
And looking for that tiny opening to leave through
In the twilight time forgot
And now I pierce that vale of discontent
Flex a grin through a glance
Yet still jaded
Hinged with hope and wonder
And hold tight to that traditional one-day-at-a-time
nonfiction

Untitled

Behold the four stained walls of the inside
Where the nightmares carry the flash of that red Utopian
sunset
Where you wilt with hunger and your eyes burn and skin
blotched
With remembrance of the smell of your first ghetto
The first stomach pain of America's freedom

Where have those restless nights of summer gone
Burning marijuana in cages of youth
Gorged on the naked blonde that was hidden in the file
cabinet
Scores of school bells disrupting oral pleasures
Vacuumed in her eyes in vacant rooms studying the human
form of rebellion
To some lone muted romance in the back of ecstasy's casket

Near the ash and coals and embers
The cricket, the frog, the locust rendition of the Southern
night
To the flesh, to the feel, to the stench of sweat
In the hemisphere of orgasm where moans are hushed by
virtue
And sleep comes to the limbs of our twisted bodies

Out into the dizzy prescription paths of a new days dawning
The quake and rattle of nerves as I awoke hung over on
clouds adrift
By no fault it was another black mountain morning
Where they pop-up like hillbilly gallery ducks
The absence of sunshine in poor pockets
With not one cleansed queer petal to palm
But I inched up the lattice of the early morning melancholy
Escaping that flaccid jewel of a moon

These streets are littered with endless and nameless prophets
Who too are lathered in the luxury of young mystery
Those who knitted garments of onions and cooked from
cauldrons of wisdom
Illuminating my conduit to destruction
Forewarning me of the biblicals' who would destroy me in
the end
It simmers up from beneath my feet swallowing me in a
cloud of longing
For I have put rusty nails in the hearts of those who love me
And I am sorry and struggle with the breaths of I love you

I'm a cold cracked hourglass
Selfish with ten fold tyrants that ignore
All while practicing sleep deprivation
In a tiny dollhouse closet where its walls are scattered with
buck-shot blood stains
Dwelling panorama shifts as if escape was the nightmare
And there were a carousel of Dalian landscapes
And there I was taking it all in
In a Jesus Christ pose with medications balanced on the tip
of my nose

Bound by the matrimony of an artificial harmony
Scouring through a trunk of my past looking for a story
book romance
Only to end medieval like two-headed fiction
Heartbroken and sobbing tombs of alcohol
With a handful of Greek tragedies
Am I the prick, thorn, or fool?
Or that vagabond of sympathy's sculptures?

And when locked in institutions
The psych
Audaciously inquiring
How do you feel today?
Are you suicidal?
There is no problem beyond
I am a drug addict
Hidden under trees of antidepressants
In bushes of sleeping pills
As for suicide
Yes!
A thousand times on paper
In the darkness of nowhere alley
And outside windows
Subsequently in conversations with my mother

Yawn…
As for politics
Don't ask
My political aspirations are debauched
Now we're choking on the victims teeth
With a leader deemed to be a warmonger…oil junkie
Promoting a science that destroys life in order to save it
I am not a martyr

Yet the penny-pushing regime stated I violated a U.S.
policy...
Concerning a Puerto Rican girl in an abandoned building

Possessing an indifferent odium for television
And undaunted regarding anyone's sex life in Hollywood
Unless I'm stranded on my knees alone
Gossip is grounds for gossip
I find myself saddened by all of this country's children
Whose parents die stitched to the woven war machines
Trapped in the fabric of this "American Puppet: Oil for
Food Foundation"
I just want to live in a decent apartment
Free to write obscenities and musical masturbations
All the while
Grinning at my loving companion behind closed doors
With such to argue into oblivion about the price of heroin
and gas

I am not much different than you
I want, what I want, what I want
Like any other American citizen
Who is poor and doesn't want to die alone

The Hangman's Guard

I know the signs of the hangman's guard
His dangling cuffs and his lazy pooch
The stern and anchor rattles at his hips
As he grinds his teeth…
Full of tobacco grains
But like a peeled plum
Soft as satin on the inside
His arms in crossbone position
Eyes of the Devil's delight
Can't fool me, can't fool the foul
Brown saliva drains from his cracked sarchasm
His fat ass gnaws away at his cheap cotton briefs
Like teething on shit
His pudgy aging face hangs, pickled under fluorescent lights

Ohh…
Big man got a gun!
Big man got a bully stopper!
Mama said he make the bad guys run
Big scary fat-cheeked plumped plum lazy pile of sidekicked
mule shit
He guards the gown of the hangman as he picks his nose
As if he's invisible only when he needs to be
Adjusting his belt and brooding in his chest
And where his boogers belong

We'll never know?

As he slowly ejaculates his pistol grip
I look him straight in the eyes
And only a mumble through the air…
You ain't got nothing on me man!
Just wheel me away like the baggage carts

———————————————————

Untitled

We slowly grazed under the neons of the street as we passed
I, the yellow prince of cadavers
Inside the spine of her stanzas
She, the host of a living dream
A haze brewed around her
As she caressed the pavement
I stood with a thousand heartbeats
Inundated...
Salisbury tongue,
As I drink my liquor from a cloud
With the sounds of immortal Chopin

In disbelief...I lazed
Hypnotized by rustic images on naked paté
She glances at me from her velvety painting
Under the skull of light
As the music swells
And my ghost heavies near her
Angel-eyed like crossing a million moons
Crescendos erupt as I imagined we touched

Time grew immaculate with her presence
With her sweet jelly banter and the practice of my ape's
ballet

Her eyes became the melancholy sensation of a cool blue
dream
The rhapsody held beasts at bay in wilted solvent springs
Sharpening my moans to smooth polar stars
Turning my heart September soft
Layers upon layers of her breath melt each minute
I felt sacrificial in deep dwelling pits of burgundy woven
skies

Sonnets burst!
As my ashes drift to the olive colored caves of her lips
Conducting each note
With dagger in hand and heart in throat
This world was beyond me
As I copulate and egress through a hole in space
The crowd applauds!

And through tar stained mascara she blinked
And was gone
As I awake
In a stained dreamy disillusion
Nothing but a cracked frame boarding torn grey canvas
Just like a crumbling sculpture
Cracking the axis
The yoke, dripping from the moon
Shaking the chandelier of stars

A million seconds of slow devastation
With one violent brush
A world of love and lust was whisked away
When the two of us never existed
Outside of the mind
The world was still in slumber

The nightmare is the awaking of dreams

Suffer Thee

I remember the last time I was in the Carolinas
Things got hot, things got strange, things got curdled
Things got stained and pointed fingers had taken blame

I went to see a show…the sounds of Iggy Pop
Dancing with the tribal youth from floor to table tops
She's jealous now like jealous not
'Cause she ain't high from morphine's drop
So she drove to where the city rots
Near that boulevard that's maimed by cops
And shops the spots for unholstered cocks
Trying to fulfill what dope cannot

I engage in the pardon that nothing's changed
As shadows rest in clouds of rain
May I partake in points of pain?
To wilt within the lethargic frame
The good die young, but their ghosts remain

This house of hearts' been burglarized
Lost my light
Dim fireflies
But candles burn
Suicide!

The clock tiptoes into the dark
God is raging—I am not
My limbs be numb like juggernauts
May my tourniquets be tied in knots

And when all is done she claimed me up
On a winding highway around two o'clock
My feet were heavy and my veins were hot
And she invites me into the open door
The light hits my face—fluorescent glow
I spoke no words and gained no luck
But her scent had scent my nose a fuck

With panties stained beneath the seat
A heart that rages a bastard's beat
Rain that slithers on the window's slant
A strong meditation where the eyes are kept
The dimming neon of nonchalance
And maybe all the weeping's wept?
Clouds have dropped where fog now sets
A grim reminder of right and wrong
The memories now skull and bone
Sets the tone, no longer longed
And stomp the ash of sing and song
So suffer thee—times ten would be nice
And hope you never see your paradise

The Doom Machine

Come take a trip on the doom machine
It mentally fucks you with a whipping psychotic
And when it's finished, it leaves the taste of a rusty spoon
It always wears that coffin expression
Of a bad trip
And it loosens your bowels like in the wake of a neglected
infant
You seizure and spasm with paranoia
Its signals lead you in circles
It only cost you this existence

Have you ever been so frightened
Your life flashes like a million flickering instances?
Your heartbeat stutters and your legs shake
Your entire body trembles with moist cheeks
And then they open that door to a thousand suffering faces
You can't help but lie to yourself
And twist your tongue in a hot knot, lying in a puddle of
lava
You gargle the marbles of trepidation
As they fall down your throat one at a time

You glance behind yourself as the steel doors slam
You can see your guardian angel hung on the wire with
hopelessness

As his wings flutter to the ground in panic
It's that chilled October chrome
As the feathers fall slowly
The sad foot stops of all the saints before him
Heaven forbid you wrestle the first "forgive me" of an ego
You might get your teeth knocked out again
And this doom machine's got no exits
Got no eject button
It thunders in its voice
And its bite is a motherfucker of death

Moon

Florescent espresso rhizomes of light
At night
Those shiny toxins
That spring forth against the sun
A neon bug light for junkies, vampires, thieves, and
nocturnal nothings

Moon

Held steady-long
Before the arm, leg or thigh
Before the awakening of reality
The human standstill
With salt rock and crystallized candies
That frozen piñata of doom

Moon

The unassailable hand holds the candle
That melts fast with fury
The high pinnacle of time
And the only earth I need

Life On The Concrete Earth

With endless connotations
Under the flaming North Star of tonight
With Neptune above and beyond
Bricked in brown bookcases
Brimming with Milton…with Blake…with Plath
And Swedenborg
Where Rimbaud can finally laugh
Through the torn pages of time revealed

I was one year down
In a life of wasted myriads
Filling the key holes of the future

Life on the concrete earth

In sands of old tombs
Like old grey cemetery haunts
With flittering dying locusts
That form shadows of Hocus Pocus
A séance of wish backs
In cursed necros
With feline hands and a sharp tiger-tooth gaze
Hungry and vengeful with tall cool strides of ego
What lives behind these eyes?
Cursed to choose

Beyond perils of light
That old crow of wicked thought
Black winged and creeping
Perched on the left side of Death
Unhinged and hugging an infinite pestilence
Nil…unspoken yet blamed

Life on the concrete earth

Lockdown onto lockdown
All eyes piercing through holes of beans
Inept escape
By phone or hand
And can't climb down with Whitman's big white beard
Tho his words will do me great
Like saints collapsing cathedrals of the unjust
Yet…I am not
And fools built the great Parthenons
Towering high in boredom
I reign
I am the king of ants
But I am starving
Dripping drooling chin down dirty toilets
Where flush roars the deep sonata
Of a forbidden knowledge
And in sinks
Where Oppenheimer grins
From a cold silver push-button monastery

I am the eyes and ears of the 21st century
Vomiting lotus petals
Under the screams that blanket light

Lights out!

And this is life on the concrete earth

A Slow Rain on Razors

A slow rain on razors
I never knew a night could cut so deep
When minutes are hours
And my only friend is an imaginary serpent that slithers on
my bed railing

This is the time of ghosts and shadows
When the paranormal twitch tacks open my eyelids
As the thunder outside strangles the walls around me
I'm harpooned by disbelief
Shutter the silence of time's second hand

Tic, Tock, Tick, Tock...
Drips slow abrasive raindrops
Outside a tiny framed window
Stained from years of grief

A slow rain on razors
Where a tiny star appears
Above a glass rooftop full of dreams
That collects in a halo and circles the compound
And projected through the skulls of brick and mortar
There was the swelling of mid-drift screams

Beyond October and leaves blown by

Time drags its belly on the barbed-wire
Where the buzzards hover around hopelessness
And a slow rain on razors makes a mind go mad

O Where Do I Weep?

O where do I weep?
Somewhere in the subconscious, known as sleep
Out in the cemeteries where the fireflies creep
In the cracks of the mind, where tears flush to seep

O where do I weep?
On those mysterious of oceans with the greatest of fleets
A heavy knock at the door, where my head has been beat
In the lap of a whore, cradled by deceit
Mocked and shamed and lynched by defeat

O where do I weep?
In my cold rusty armor, penetrated by streets
On the beautiful pastures where I slaughter sheep
In the pit of the vein where the needle's too deep
With the sound of Death's trumpets that follow my feet
And stagger my shadows where strangers don't speak

O where do I weep?
In the fiction of danger where truth can't be seen
In a soup kitchen line, waiting to feast
In a tiny glass house where pebbles break deep
On a cloud belly-up with pharmaceutical treats

O where do I weep?

Lost in the shadows my eyes sewn to sheets
In a shroud of flesh dancing on teeth
On the side streets of December, searching for heat
Trapped in a cube, to rot or retreat?

The Fall of the House of the Fascist

I've noticed there's a huge problem in this house
Beyond the rice and bean shortage
The Nuremberg Rally is on TV way too often
And he curses for it to be in color
In his chamber den, a Confederate flag and a Nazi flag
In a juxtaposed position
He cuts Colby cheese with a replica Hitler Youth dagger
And sips on some Black Label
Although, the authentic Youth dagger is housed
In his race-box, next to a copy of The Turner Diaries

What's a young boy to do?

Got anti-Semitism spilt all over the kitchen table!
Got the Luftwaffe bangin' on the front door!
Got several Axis troops bombarding my escape hatch in the
basement
I saw him building guns again
Saw him trading with the rebels
Saw my brother getting nauseous from the nerve gas

I was more of an anarchist I guess?

But I was crushed a few years after King Alfonso left the
house

And I could still see the smoke
It blinded me for years
Choked on some mustard gas Mom made
Her tongue in knots and her ideas held hostage

Friends would sometimes come by
With their mouths ajar—drooling
Fixated on a poisoned history lesson
By a drunken, askewed militant
Who wanted so bad to take a shot at Charlie in the bush
But the shit cooled down by the time he could enlist
Can only fantasize now
In books and photographs
Perched proud on his recliner made of human bone
A warmonger who watched bootleg movies of Jewish
atrocities

Bedazzled!

Now what the hell is going on here?
Hear you marching up and down the hall
Goose stepping back and forth
In those imported leather boots

I'm one scared son of a bitch!

Screaming in a (not so fluent) German tongue
With a twist of slant-eyed Kamikaze
But the tone was so abrasive

This war was like a cup of tea
Sometimes hot, sometimes cold

I guess I'll hide away
As passive as Stonehenge
Scrawl in these notebooks
And turn on the punk rock
I've been annexed in my own bedroom
I'm gonna end up in the Belsen bathroom
Hidden behind the washing machine
Gonna pull a coup with my brother
And bounce from this Blitzkrieg snake pit

Dance Midnight Dance

Dance midnight dance!
in a shimmering shade of decadence
the sweetest wine of a Dionysian feast
the shuttered eyes of a hero's defeat
that shivering curl of the spine that only Poe could create
with poignant deceit

Dance midnight dance!
and blotch the pit of the sun
to perch your ass upon the bluest moon
and find you ravaged and hungry with wounds
Fuck their lies! Fuck their claims!
and pierce these walls like Jene Genet!

Dance midnight dance!
to tribute these high tides in the name of Hart Crane
opium tongue, opium stains
the pillars can't hold what the pillars can't contain
yet the pillow softens the petals stars
with memories lost and memories named

the drama we bring twists and curls around the weight of
the world
the weight of a page full of emotional words
as a fat woman snarls at the youth of a girl

under a streetlight, trading pussy for pearls

Dance midnight dance!
and bathe in the flames
like the wolf that devours what's yet to be maimed
feed the words to the poet like a vampire's vein
the words are just paintings without the frame
and symbols are allegories
her hands be bound but never boring
the passing headlights tainted her delights
and never goes gently to the dying goodnights
as Lord Calvert rests on her breath
where Hemingway and Bukowski sat
and ate the beans from Kerouac
to the sound of Thompson's cannon crack

Dance midnight dance!
until your burning bosom inspires
from the alleyway fires and sacrificial pyres
the vixen laughs and curses my speech
and pisses where I plant my feet
and the poetry strengthens to become much more
like the lacquer on the shithouse door
in the whistling winds of whippoorwhills
and shadowed by wings of daffodils
to leaves of graveyards where death may come
and Lazarus won't weep no more

So you dance midnight dance!
and your dreams will become your tears unborn
and suffer he who loves a whore
and fights to write and become much more
like a bitch in heat outside my door

she pronounced her brim is never full
and copulates as her lust is born
so I send these dreadful nights away
and escape the stars that doom to bloom
and scream from life's pedestal
as I claw the hand that stitches the wound

And Poetry Again Nails Its Coffin

As I come to my senses
Pulling my fiery chemical beast to the broken shoulder of
Truth Highway
Smoking…
Allowing the ghosts of family and friends to glance in the
rearview
Decelerating this disease-ridden, disembodied warhead…
To rest under funnels of purple clouds
Chemical Valley

Sanctioning white plutonium gases
As they steam hot with alacrity
From the vehement tar beneath my wheels
With screw-daddy eyes that render a soul restless forever
Lies of clad suited fixtures
And the night reaches out its quivering unrest
And all the stars are stitched into beliefs…

Here we dream of cities and streets
Landscapes beyond this unnatural disaster
Living like cloned machines of the body
A twisted tongue that shelters granite poetry
The only future is the word
As strong as the one that created God
And the ones that had failed before him

Who are the martyrs of prose?
With extinct forms I trouble to discern
They walk behind the moons
Forever without peace
Bring on the slow shift of change
With that tarantula thought
That can't conceive a poisoned image

A twenty-four hour waltz of the dead
Under the chandelier of oiled sky
To candelabra sunrise
Paints the dew of a sleepy faced antic
Of a rabid morphine infused heart
Imbedded with restless mad screaming
Condemned to impale myself upon daggers

By medications upon medications
A locomotive pharmaceutical alleyway
To those countertops of Clorox-circled cleanliness
Some blind doctor's robotic right hand
Of a poppy prescription pad
We have become the newest soldiers
And the battle forever rages
Like my pen…

And poetry again nails its coffin

Untitled

Beyond the valleys of sobriety
Are the dirt roads to excess
Full of insecurities
And vicious stray inhumanities
Filthy and rabid with excitement
In a world all our own

The sex was the most outrageous
And the addiction
Was the sex

We were prisoners of adventure's tormented sister
Leaps and bounds beyond numbness
Howling under the nightmare of the stars
The fears of who we were kept us prowling at lull
Thirsting for the blood of the spoon

Driving junked-out caskets
That ran on human remains
Ventilated the pain and suffering

On nights like this the world has got to suffer
Some host would fall victim to vampire-like deeds

We praise the prostitutions and acts of random anarchy!

We welcome you to graffiti the souls of common men!

But somewhere in the time and space of dread
Peaceful words are spoken in bundles of echoes
And remorse has a mighty sword
Double edged in empathy…

Sculpting Fire

From the bottom of an impoverished void, I ask…
Mend my wings, me, and my mind
Caress my skull with ease

Until the essence of my true soul can be revealed

Beneath the darkness of solitude
You could find me
Wallowing the depths with drunken shadows
Stoned like a vulture, from the foothills of Golgotha

Until this moment
I'm ready to ascend
Ready to release that anchored spirit that bounds me
Ready to find myself…
Safe as Milk

I know the portrait of permanent scars
And what's done is done
And to whom?
Who am I?
I've grown accustomed to the delusional void
Becoming my own light at the end of the tunnel

Goodbye Sins!

Left to drive a quivering demise down the streets of insanity
One wheel and to die
Yet failed to

I return with words and woes of teeth chattering density
With reverent eyes
That belongs to my first child-like symmetry

To be bathed in the brightest light imaginable

No more hysteria, no more fear
No more bodies to trample on in the midst of war
No more dancing ceremoniously on nails for the pleasures
of pain
Galloping through depression

No more knocking the dust from the arms of lonesome allies
No more riding serpents down the streets of endless frosted
cement
No more using maggots to clean my wounds or stealing
beyond the gates of the wealthy
No more feeding from the necks of prescription trashcans
Starving like a vampire under every hyper moon

Yearning to lodge…

Upside down with disease-stricken bats in the realms of
shooting galleries

No more cradling swarms of whores in the uterus of space
Dark with pubic stars

Goodbye Sins!

I perched on the granite muscle
Into that vein of life that gives…to see where I'm published
when I become defunct
I'll be staggering slow on lucid clouds of pearl, wearing a
cherubic mask

Innocent but not…distressed in adventure
As the classical gas of my old soul creeps open like a
skulker being born
But one who leans on an anguished crutch with crow
scattering emotions

Take away those dark cloud ecstasies that mimicked down
like saliva raindrops
Open to peace in some holy silence
Letting the panic collect in the rusty hubcaps of equilateral
heights
With that awkward glance of my watery reflection in
pulsating circles

I lie at the doorstep of my birth, and beyond my graveyards
Transcending familiar gardens engulfed in vivid
hallucinations

Onto abandoned apartments with only a sofa carcass
One that held a hundred grave robbing heroes before me
Hovering two feet high above its pillows on an intravenous
bliss
Sprouting Satori-calloused tracks in a tepid left arm

Allergic and sneezing through ghost-bubble corners of dust
Near cobweb saddled panhandles
Bordering oceans of chipped wallpaper that crashes into the
island of rat droppings

Within the screams of burning tissue, beneath the tattered
sleeves of flannel
Lie the marks of…been there, done that…tattoos

Now…close your eyes, if only for a moment…
Relax your shoulders and breathe in peace
and exhale transgression…

Goodbye Sins!

Once again well exited, like downtown businessmen
Back and forth…akin to Chinese fire drill oxfords
With cheap suits, bearing the essence of cheap cologne

Demonized and victim to the part of the dead father

Lost mother…white trash disaster

Giving up withered heart mournings of disrobed winters
On to the naked fruitful stings of summer
Strung-out on one thousand remembers
With its post traumatic haunts and its grand and elegant
moods to die for

Expressing my deepest thoughts to a girl
Who was smooth and soft like sand dunes
With surprising gullet-like openings
Slippery and slick—seductive

Then back out, to either end of the tilted city
Dodging cops and crucibles alike, to share with you
staggering intensities
Living from stolen pockets, till I emptied, then repeat

Finding myself again in an open-hallowed reality
Caressing the stains of a cold jail cell floor, sick and
withering
With bending bones, growling, craving the chaos,
And chiseled into a clown by a broken crown

And I menaced in the face of sobriety for days

Until I found myself blistered and mounted on the top of the
red skull of empty buildings
Watching them squirm at daybreak
While the city burned
My pupils dilated…I imagined rest in some peaceful
sanctuary

Fallen now to the narrow blue islands of an escape
Wondering what a Sunday of hope could bring
And dress it in pure white
Like a savior, robed in genius, bearing a crucifix, with one
giant hand
Faded pale skin
Wrinkled with knowledge to sweep me away
Back to innocence

Goodbye Sins!

I dance the dance of pranksters
As fools shrug and tumble in ruin
Mistakes arranged in landmine formation in dirt

Missing the days when I was asphyxiated in my teenage
bedroom
Stoned on art and the sounds of crass lament

My poet awakened in mesmerizing cycles

Roaming around with residents and their nine gigabytes of
RAM intellect
And one million tongue-tied pronunciations
The twist and curl of cursed linguistics

I could only revolt against the asinine evolution

Yet suffering has long taken its place
I viewed them all from a trance with kaleidoscope
spectacles
In the midst of my thinly disguised character

So now I say…
Take my gun take my antidepressants
My sleeping pills

Take all my drugs
Take all my confusion
All of my emotions and queer poetry
And stick it up your ass

The time has come to free myself from you
And all fiery burdens

Let it rain down unsullied daydreams cultivating flocks of
new-fangled images

I give back my greedy hands and wilted nights hidden in the
cold bellies of cellars
Diamond black in mud clad boots, wet with boot hill blisters
I want to become as humble as an infant, blinded by the
bliss of hunting Easter eggs
Carrying the comforts of a god in my pockets

My road to excess has led to my destruction…Blake!

And like the raging waters I move forward
Wounded by the pierce of septicemia
My pen and fist to perdition
Nothing more at stake

Only a tongue that comes to you in twisted ranting

Goodbye Sins!

Over and over I sculpt this inferno of thought
Open the skull and stir
Rummage through the bones of before
I capture serendipity with mistake traps, on roads of
yesterday
Beckoning you to create your own blissful paradise
And maybe see me in the end

Write your own polemic pages to wade through the depth
and enlighten
Flow toward your own celestial emotions
Take rebellion in your own eyes, on paper, through streets
Or that long perennial path of discovery
Learn by the sword of every mistake

Blunder into enchantment
And drown as I did

Take from my scared pages
Revolutionized in a few minutes of poetry

Now you may walk away

Goodbye Sins!

www.ingramcontent.com/pod-product-compliance
Lightning Source LLC
Chambersburg PA
CBHW032059040426
42449CB00007B/1138